From the Bible-Teaching Ministry of

CHARLES R. SWINDOLL

HOPE
for the Hurting

LifeMaps

Insight for Living

HOPE FOR THE HURTING
A LifeMaps Book

From the Bible-Teaching Ministry of Charles R. Swindoll

Charles R. Swindoll has devoted his life to the clear, practical teaching and application of God's Word and His grace. A pastor at heart, Chuck has served as senior pastor to congregations in Texas, Massachusetts, and California. He currently pastors Stonebriar Community Church in Frisco, Texas, but Chuck's listening audience extends far beyond a local church body. As a leading program in Christian broadcasting, *Insight for Living* airs in major Christian radio markets around the world, reaching people groups in languages they can understand. Chuck's extensive writing ministry has also served the body of Christ worldwide and his leadership as president and now chancellor of Dallas Theological Seminary has helped prepare and equip a new generation for ministry. Chuck and Cynthia, his partner in life and ministry, have four grown children and ten grandchildren.

Published By:
IFL Publishing House
A Division of Insight for Living
Post Office Box 251007
Plano, Texas 75025-1007

Hope for the Hurting was collaboratively developed by Creative Ministries of Insight for Living.
Writer for chapters two and four: Derrick G. Jeter, Th.M., Dallas Theological Seminary
Editor in Chief: Cynthia Swindoll, President, Insight for Living
Executive Vice President: Wayne Stiles, Th.M., D.Min., Dallas Theological Seminary
Theological Editor: John Adair, Th.M., Ph.D., Dallas Theological Seminary
Content Editor: Amy L. Snedaker, B.A., English, Rhodes College
Copy Editors: Jim Craft, M.A., English, Mississippi College
    Kathryn Merritt, M.A., English, Hardin-Simmons University
Project Coordinator, Creative Ministries: Melanie Munnell, M.A., Humanities,
    The University of Texas at Dallas
Project Coordinator, Communications: Sarah Magnoni, A.A.S.,
    University of Wisconsin
Proofreader: Paula McCoy, B.A., English, Texas A&M University-Commerce
Cover Design: Kari Pratt, B.A., Commercial Art, Southwestern Oklahoma State University
Production Artist: Nancy Gustine, B.F.A., Advertising Art, University of North Texas

Chapter one was adapted from "Hope Beyond Suffering: How We Can Smile Through Suffering," chapter two in Charles R. Swindoll's book *Hope Again: When Life Hurts and Dreams Fade* (Dallas: Word Publishing, 1996), 11–23.

Chapter three was adapted from "What Job Teaches Us about Ourselves," chapter twenty-one in Charles R. Swindoll's book *Job: A Man of Heroic Endurance* (Nashville: W Publishing Group, 2004), 321–38.

Unless otherwise identified, Scripture quotations used in this book are from the *New American Standard Bible*® (NASB). Copyright © 1960, 1962, 1963, 1968, 1971, 1972, 1973, 1975, 1977, 1995 by The Lockman Foundation, La Habra, California. All rights reserved. Used by permission. (www.lockman.org)

Scripture quotations marked (MSG) are from *The Message*. Copyright © 1993, 1994, 1995, 1996, 2000, 2001, 2002 by Eugene H. Peterson. All rights reserved. Used by permission of NavPress Publishing Group.

An effort has been made to locate sources and obtain permission where necessary for the quotations used in this LifeMaps book. In the event of any unintentional omission, a modification will gladly be incorporated in future printings.

ISBN: 978-1-57972-887-8
Printed in the United States of America

Table of Contents

A Letter from Chuck

Suffering. Pain. Hurt.

Look at those words. Just the mere letters on the page are enough to send shivers of sadness and dread down anyone's spine. Why? Because all of us know the awful, hollow ache of suffering—the death of dreams and loved ones, the pain of rejection and physical infirmities, the agonizing questions of "why?" and "where's God?"

The old saying is true: you cannot get out of life alive. But equally true is the inescapable fact that you cannot escape suffering. It is simply part of life on this sin-saturated planet. But that doesn't mean we have to go through life with a hangdog expression, moaning and grumbling. Not at all! We can live with hope, even in the midst of our deepest hurts. In fact, we *must* live with hope or we can't live at all. Without hope our spirits die . . . with hope we can face any hardship. Here's why:

- Hope points us to the light when we are trapped in a dark tunnel of misery.

- Hope buoys our spirits when we are drowning in discouragement.

- Hope dulls the edge of panic when we lose our way.

- Hope gives us courage to press on regardless of crippling disease or lingering illness.

- Hope reminds us that God is still in control when fears creep into our lives.

- Hope tells us we have a future when we find ourselves unemployed or divorced.

- Hope encourages us with the truth that life endures beyond death when we stand at the graveside of a loved one.

Simply put, nothing helps like hope when we are hurting.

That's why Insight for Living created this *LifeMaps* book. Rather than trying to answer every question about suffering, *Hope for the Hurting* instead will put steel into your soul when you suffer. It will remind you that hope is available when you hurt and assure you that you don't suffer alone. It will also point out valuable lessons you can learn about yourself and offer counsel on how to answer others who suffer. In a word, this book will help point you to the source of hope in suffering: Jesus Christ.

Hope. Confidence. Healing. Aren't you ready to put these words back onto the page of your life? This is a good place to start.

Charles R. Swindoll

At its heart, a map is the distillation of the experience of travelers—those who have journeyed in the past and recorded their memories in the form of pictures and symbols. The map represents the cumulative wisdom of generations of travelers, put together for the benefit of those now wishing to make that same journey.

To undertake a journey with a map is therefore to rely on the wisdom of the past. It is to benefit from the hard-won knowledge of those who have explored the unknown and braved danger in order to serve those who will follow in their footsteps. Behind the lines and symbols of the map lie countless personal stories—stories the map itself can never tell. Yet sometimes those stories need to be told, just as the hard-won insights of coping with traveling can encourage, inspire, and assist us.[1]

—Alister E. McGrath

Welcome to LifeMaps

On a journey, the important thing is not speed as much as it is *direction*.

But sometimes heading the right way requires some guidance. Think about it. You would never set out on a long road trip without first making sure you knew which direction to go, right? You'd consult a map. For many people, the journey toward a deeper and more meaningful relationship with God lies along new or unfamiliar ground. They need directions; they need a map. And, even with a map, sometimes you can still get lost. When you do, it's the locals who know best — those who have been down the same roads. That's why this book is designed to be completed in concert with someone else. Wise friends or counselors can encourage us in our spiritual growth and help us avoid pitfalls along our paths.

Using LifeMaps

LifeMaps provides opportunities for individuals to interact with the Bible in different settings and on several levels, depending upon your particular needs or interests. *LifeMaps* also places a tool in the hands of pastors and other Christian leaders, helping them guide others along a journey of spiritual growth through the study and application of the Bible.

For Individuals

You can use *LifeMaps* in your personal devotionals to gain God's perspective on a particular area of Christian living. In addition to offering engaging chapters to read, *LifeMaps* can further your journey of spiritual growth with the help of penetrating questions and opportunities for personal application.

LifeMaps can also serve as a first step to healing or resolving an issue that continues to plague you. Read, reflect, answer the questions, and then contact a competent, mature, godly man or woman to discuss the topic as it relates to your personal situation. This individual can be a pastor, a counselor, a friend, or even one of our staff here at Insight for Living in Pastoral Ministries. (See page 83 for information on how to contact Insight for Living.) This step is an essential part of the journey.

For Pastors and Counselors

LifeMaps is designed to guide individuals through an engaging, in-depth study of the Word of God, freeing you to help them apply the truths in even more specific and personal ways. As a vital first step in the counseling process, each volume lays a solid, biblical, theological, and practical foundation upon which you can build. Encouraging individuals to work through the book on their own allows them the time necessary for personal reflection and education while enabling you to target your ministry of personal interaction and discipleship to their particular needs.

For Groups

LifeMaps can serve as a curriculum for home Bible studies, Sunday school classes, and accountability or discipleship groups. Each book in the series contains enough material for group discussion of key questions and noteworthy passages. *LifeMaps* can also foster meaningful interaction for pastors, elders, staff, and Christian leaders.

Suggestions for Study

Whether you use *LifeMaps* in a group, in a counseling setting, in the classroom, or for personal study, we trust it will prove to be an invaluable guide as you seek deeper intimacy with God and growth in godliness. In any setting, the following suggestions will make *LifeMaps* more beneficial for you.

- Begin each chapter with prayer, asking God to teach you through His Word and to open your heart to the self-discovery afforded by the questions and text.

- Read the chapters with pen in hand. Underline any thoughts, quotes, or verses that stand out to you. Use the pages provided at the end of each section to record any questions you may have, especially if you plan to meet with others for discussion.

- Have your Bible handy. In chapters 2 and 4, you'll be prompted to read relevant sections of Scripture and answer questions related to the topic.

- As you complete each chapter, close with prayer, asking God to apply the wisdom and principles to your life by His Holy Spirit. Then watch God work! He may bring people and things into your life that will challenge your attitudes and actions. You may gain new insight about the world and your faith. You may find yourself applying this new wisdom in ways you never expected.

May God's Word illumine your path as you begin your journey. We trust that this volume in the *LifeMaps* series will be a trustworthy guide to learning and to your spiritual growth.

HOPE
for the Hurting

Chapter 1

Hope beyond Suffering

We don't look alike. We don't act alike. We don't dress alike. We have different tastes in the food we eat, the books we read, the cars we drive, and the music we enjoy. You like opera; I like country. You like rock climbing; I like Harleys. We have diverse backgrounds, goals, and motivations. We work at different jobs, and we enjoy different hobbies. We hold to a variety of philosophies and politics. We have our own unique convictions on child-rearing and education. Our weights vary. Our heights vary. So does the color of our skin.

In short . . . everybody's different.

But there's one thing we all have in common: we all know what it means to hurt.

Suffering is a universal language. Tears are the same for Jews or Muslims or Christians, for white or black or brown, for children or adults or the elderly. When life hurts and our dreams fade, we may express our anguish in different ways, but each one of us knows the sting of pain and heartache . . . disease and disaster . . . trials and sufferings.

Joseph Parker, a great preacher of yesteryear, once said to a group of aspiring young ministers, "Preach to the suffering and you will never lack a congregation. There is a broken heart in every pew." I couldn't agree more.

Truly, suffering is the common thread in all our garments.

This has been true since the beginning, when sin entered the world and Adam and Eve were driven from the garden. It shouldn't surprise us, therefore, that when the apostle Peter wrote his first letter to fellow believers scattered throughout much of Asia Minor, he focused on the one subject that drew all of them together. Suffering.

These people were being singed by the same flames of persecution that would take the apostle's life in just a few years. Their circumstances were the bleakest imaginable. Yet Peter didn't try to pump them up with positive thinking. Instead, he gently reached his hand to their chins and lifted their faces skyward—so they could see beyond their circumstances to their celestial calling.

> Peter, an apostle of Jesus Christ,
> To those who reside as aliens, scattered
> throughout Pontus, Galatia, Cappadocia,
> Asia, and Bithynia, who are chosen
> according to the foreknowledge of God
> the Father, by the sanctifying work
> of the Spirit, to obey Jesus Christ and
> be sprinkled with His blood: May grace
> and peace be yours in fullest measure.
> (1 Peter 1:1–2)

The men and women to whom Peter wrote knew what it was like to be away from home, not by choice but by force. Persecuted for their faith, they had been pushed out into a world that was not only unfamiliar but hostile.

Warren Wiersbe, in a fine little book titled *Be Hopeful*, said this about the recipients of the letter:

> The important thing for us to know about these "scattered strangers" is that they were going through a time of suffering and persecution. At least fifteen times in this letter, Peter referred to suffering; and he used eight different Greek words to do so. Some of these Christians were suffering because they were living godly lives and doing what was good and right. . . . Others were suffering reproach for the name of Christ . . . and being railed at by unsaved people. . . . Peter wrote to encourage them to be good witnesses to their persecutors, and to remember that their suffering would lead to glory.[1]

Take another look at the beginning of that last sentence: "Peter wrote to encourage them to be good witnesses to their persecutors." It is so easy to read that. It is even easier to preach it. But it is *extremely* difficult to do it. If you have ever been mistreated, you know what a great temptation it is to retaliate, to defend yourself, to fight back, to treat the other person as he or she has treated you. Peter wanted to encourage his fellow believers to put pain in perspective and find hope beyond their suffering.

While most of us are not afflicted by horrible persecution for our faith, we do know what it means to face various forms of suffering, pain, disappointment, and grief. Thankfully, in the letter of 1 Peter, we can find comfort and consolation for our own brand of suffering. Just as this treasured document spoke to the believers scattered in Pontius or Galatia or Cappadocia or Asia, so it speaks to us today, no matter where we are in the world.

The first good news Peter gave us is that we are "chosen by God." What a helpful reminder! We aren't just thrown on this earth like dice tossed across a table. We are sovereignly and lovingly placed here for a purpose, having been chosen by God. His choosing us was "according to [His] foreknowledge . . . by the sanctifying work of the Spirit . . . [that we may] obey Jesus Christ . . . [having been] sprinkled with His blood" (1 Peter 1:2). Powerful words!

God has given us a purpose for our existence, a reason to go on, even though that existence includes tough times. By our living through suffering, we become sanctified — in other words, set apart for the glory of God. We gain perspective. We grow deeper. We grow up!

Can you imagine going through such times without Jesus Christ? I can't. But frankly, that's what most people do. They face those debilitating fears and sleepless nights in the hospital, without Christ. They struggle with a wayward teenager, without Christ. Alone, they endure the awful words from a mate, "I don't want to live with you any longer. I want my freedom. I don't love you anymore. I'm gone." And they go through it all without Christ.

For souls like these, life is one painful sting after another. Just imagining what life must be like without Christ, I am surprised that more people who live without hope don't take their own lives. As appalled as I am by Jack Kevorkian and his death-on-demand philosophy, I am not surprised. What surprises me is that more people don't simply put an end to it all.

Yet if we will only believe and ask, a full measure of God's grace and peace is available to any of us. By the wonderful, prevailing mercy of God, we can find purpose in the scattering and sadness of our lives. We cannot only deal with suffering but rejoice through it. Though our pain and our disappointment and the details of our suffering may differ, there is an abundance of God's grace and peace available to each one of us.

These truths form the skeleton of strong doctrine. But unless the truths are fleshed out, they remain hard and bony and difficult to embrace. Knowing this, Peter reminded his readers of all they have to cling to so that they can actually rejoice in times of suffering, drawing on God's grace and peace in fullest measure.

Rejoicing through Hard Times

As I read and ponder Peter's first letter, I find six reasons why we as believers can rejoice through hard times and experience hope beyond suffering.

We Have a Living Hope

> Blessed be the God and Father of our Lord Jesus Christ, who according to His great mercy has caused us to be born again to a living hope through the resurrection of Jesus Christ from the dead. (1 Peter 1:3)

As difficult as some pages of our life may be, nothing that occurs to us on this earth falls into the category of "the final chapter." That chapter will not be completed until we arrive in heaven and step into the presence of the living God. Our final meeting is not with the antagonist in our life's story but with the author Himself.

"Who can mind the journey," asked the late, great Bible teacher James M. Gray, "when the road leads home?"

How can we concern ourselves that much with what happens on this temporary planet when we know that it is all leading us to our eternal destination? Peter called that our "living hope," and he reminded us that it is based on the resurrection of Jesus Christ. If God brought His Son through the most painful trials and back from the pit of death itself, certainly He can bring us through whatever we face in this world, no matter how deep that pit might seem at the time.

Do you realize how scarce hope is to those without Christ? One cynical writer, H. L. Mencken, an American newspaperman during the early half of the twentieth century, referred to hope as "a pathological belief in the occurrence of the impossible." [2]

To the unsaved, hope is nothing more than mental fantasy, like wishing upon a star. It's that kind of Disneyland hope that says, "I sure hope I win the lottery." "I hope my boy comes home someday." "I hope everything works out OK." That's not a living hope. That's wishful thinking.

But those who are "born again" in the Lord Jesus Christ have been promised a living hope through His resurrection from the dead.

So if you want to smile through your tears, if you want to rejoice through times of suffering, just keep reminding yourself that, as a Christian, what you're going through isn't the end of the story . . . it's simply the rough journey that leads to the right destination.

Hope is "like an anchor," Warren Wiersbe said. "Our hope in Christ stabilizes us in the storms of life . . . but unlike an anchor . . . it does not hold us back."[3]

We Have a Permanent Inheritance

> Blessed be the God and Father of our
> Lord Jesus Christ, who according to
> His great mercy has caused us . . .
> to obtain an inheritance which is
> imperishable and undefiled and will not
> fade away, reserved in heaven for you.
> (1 Peter 1:3–4)

We also can rejoice through suffering because we have a permanent inheritance—a secure home in heaven. And our place there is reserved under the safekeeping—the constant, omnipotent surveillance—of almighty God. Nothing can destroy it, defile it, diminish it, or displace it. Isn't that a great relief?

Have you ever had the disconcerting experience of finding someone else in the theater or airplane seat you had reserved? You hold the proper ticket, but someone else is in your seat. At best it's awkward; at worst it can lead to an embarrassing confrontation.

Have you ever made guaranteed reservations at your favorite hotel for a nonsmoking room and arrived late at night to find they have given it to someone else? What a disappointment! You give them your guaranteed reservation number and they punch endless information into the computer, then they look at you as though you've just landed from Mars. Your heart sinks. You force a smile and ask to speak to the manager. He comes out, stares at the same computer screen, then gives you the same look with a slightly deeper frown. "Sorry," he says. "There must be some kind of mistake."

Well, that's not going to happen in heaven! God will not look at you like, "Now, what did you say your name was again?" The living God will ultimately welcome you home to your permanent, reserved inheritance. Your name is on the door.

I don't know what that does to you, but it sure gives me a reason to rejoice. The more difficult life gets on this earth, the better heaven sounds.

We Have a Divine Protection

> [We] are protected by the power of God, through faith for a salvation ready to be revealed in the last time. (1 Peter 1:5)

Under heaven's lock and key, we are protected by the most efficient security system available: the power of God. There is no way we will be lost in the process of suffering. No disorder, no disease, not even death itself can weaken or threaten God's ultimate protection over our lives. No matter what the calamity, no matter what the disappointment or depth of pain, no matter what kind of destruction occurs in our bodies at the time of death, our souls are divinely protected.

Our world is filled with warfare, with atrocities, with terrorism. Think of those men and women whose lives were shattered in an instant on that September 2001 morning in New York City, in Washington, D.C., and in a gentle pasture in Pennsylvania when the world blew up around them. What happens in such times of tragic calamities? Is our eternal inheritance destroyed with our bodies? Absolutely not. Even through the most horrible of deaths, He who made us from the dust of the earth protects us by His power and promises to deliver us to our eternal destination.

"God stands between you and all that menaces your hopes or threatens your eternal welfare," biblical scholar James Moffatt wrote. "The protection of the faithful here is entirely and directly the work of God." [4]

Two words will help you cope when you run low on hope: *accept* and *trust*.

Accept the mystery of hardship, suffering, misfortune, or mistreatment. Don't try to understand it or explain it. Accept it. Then, deliberately *trust* God to protect you by His power from this very moment to the dawning of eternity.

We Have a Developing Faith

> In this you greatly rejoice, even though
> now for a little while, if necessary,
> you have been distressed by various
> trials, so that the proof of your faith,
> being more precious than gold which
> is perishable, even though tested by
> fire, may be found to result in praise
> and glory and honor at the revelation of
> Jesus Christ. (1 Peter 1:6–7)

Here is the first of several references to rejoicing in Peter's letter. The words *even though* indicate that joy is unconditional. It does not depend on the circumstances surrounding us. And don't overlook the fact that this joy comes *in spite of* our suffering, not because of it, as some who glorify suffering would have us believe. We don't rejoice because times are hard; we rejoice in spite of the fact that they are hard.

These verses also reveal three significant things about trials.

First, *trials are often necessary*, proving the genuineness of our faith and, at the same time, teaching us humility. Trials reveal our own helplessness. They put us on our face before God. They make us realistic. Or, as C. S. Lewis wrote, "[Pain] plants the flag of truth within the fortress of a rebel soul."[5] When rebels are smacked by reality, it's amazing how quickly humility replaces rigidity.

Second, *trials are distressing*, teaching us compassion so that we never make light of another's test or cruelly force others to smile while enduring it.

How unfair to trivialize another person's trial by comparing what he or she is going through with what someone else has endured. Even if you have gone through something you think is twice as difficult, comparison doesn't comfort. It doesn't help the person who has lost a child to hear that you endured the loss of two.

Express your sympathy and weep with the one who is suffering. Put your arm around him or her. Don't reel off a lot of verses. Don't try to make that hurting person pray with you or sing with you if he or she is not ready to do that. Feel what that person is feeling. Walk quietly and compassionately in his or her shoes.

Third, *trials come in various forms*. The word *various* comes from an interesting Greek term, *poikolos*, which means "variegated" or "many-colored."[6] We also get the term *polka dot* from it. Trials come in a variety of forms and colors. They are different, just as we are different. Something that would hardly affect you might knock the slats out from under me—and vice versa. But God offers special grace to match every shade of sorrow.

Paul wrote of a thorn in the flesh in 2 Corinthians 12, and he prayed three times for God to remove it. "No," said God, "I'm not taking it away." Finally Paul said, "I've learned to trust in You, Lord, I've learned to live with it." It was then that God said, "My grace is sufficient for that thorn." He matched the color of the test with the color of grace.

This variety of trials is like different temperature settings on God's furnace. The settings are adjusted to burn off our dross, to temper us, or to soften us according to what meets our highest need. It is in God's refining fire that the authenticity of our faith is revealed. And the purpose of these fiery ordeals is that we may come forth as purified gold, a shining likeness of the Lord Jesus Christ Himself. That glinting likeness is what ultimately gives glory and praise and honor to our Savior.

We Have an Unseen Savior

> And though you have not seen Him,
> you love Him, and though you do not
> see Him now, but believe in Him, you
> greatly rejoice with joy inexpressible
> and full of glory. (1 Peter 1:8)

Keep in mind that the context of this verse is suffering. So we know that Peter is not serving up an inconsequential, theological *hors d'oeuvre*. He's giving us solid meat we can sink our teeth into. He's telling us that our Savior is standing alongside us in that furnace. Our Savior is there even though we can't see Him.

You don't have to see someone to love that person. The blind mother has never seen her children, but she loves them. You don't have to see someone to believe in him or her. Believers today have never seen a physical manifestation of the Savior—we have not visibly seen

Him walking among us—but we love Him nevertheless. In times of trial, we sense He is there, and that causes us to "greatly rejoice" with inexpressible joy.

Some, like the struggling, reflective disciple Thomas, need to see and touch Jesus in order to believe. But Jesus said, "Blessed are they who did not see, and yet believed" (John 20:29). Even though we can't see Jesus standing beside us in our trials, He is there—just as He was when Shadrach, Meshach, and Abednego were thrown into the fiery furnace and survived unharmed (Daniel 3:19–30).

We Have a Guaranteed Deliverance

> [Because you greatly rejoice, you obtain] as the outcome of your faith the salvation of your souls. (1 Peter 1:9)

How can we rejoice through our pain? How can we have hope beyond our suffering? Because we have a living hope, we have a permanent inheritance, divine protection, a developing faith, an unseen Savior, and a guaranteed deliverance.

This isn't the kind of delivery the airlines promise you when you check your bags. ("Guaranteed arrival. No problem.") I'll never forget a trip I took a few years ago. I went to Canada for a conference with plans to be there for eight days. Thanks to the airline, I only had my clothes for the last two! When I finally got my luggage, I noticed the tags on them were all marked "Berlin." ("Guaranteed arrival. No problem." They just don't guarantee when or where the bags will arrive!) That's why we now see so many people boarding airplanes with a carry-on bag rolling behind them. "Don't check all your bags," these folks are saying, "because they probably won't get there when you do!"

But when it comes to spiritual delivery, Christians never have to worry. God guarantees deliverance of our souls, which includes not only a deliverance from our present sin but the glorification of our physical bodies as well. Rejoice! You're going to get there — guaranteed.

Rejoicing, not Resentment

When we suffer, only Christ's perspective can replace our resentment with rejoicing. I've seen it happen in hospital rooms. I've seen it happen in families. I've seen it happen in my own life.

Our whole perspective changes when we catch a glimpse of the purpose of Christ in it all. Take away Christ's perspective, and our suffering becomes a bitter, terrible experience.

Nancy and Ed Huizinga in Grand Rapids, Michigan, know all about this. In December 1995, while they were at church rehearsing for the annual Christmas Festival of Lights program, their home burned to the ground. But that wasn't their only tragedy that year. Just three months earlier, Nancy's longtime friend, Barb Post, a widow with two children, had died of cancer. Nancy and Ed had taken her two children, Jeff and Katie, into their home as part of their family, something they had promised Barb they would do. So when Ed and Nancy's house burned to the ground just before Christmas, it wasn't just their home that was lost; it was the new home of two teenagers who had already lost their mother and father.

As circumstances unfolded, irony went to work. The tragedy that forced the Huizingas from their home allowed Jeff and Katie to move back to theirs. Since their home had not yet been sold following their mother's death, they and the Huizinga family moved in there the night after the fire.

On the following Saturday, neighbors organized a party to sift through the ashes and search for anything of value that might have survived. One of the first indications they received of God's involvement in their struggle came as a result of that search. Somehow a piece of paper survived. On it were these words: "Contentment: realizing that God has already provided everything we need for our present happiness."

To Nancy and Ed, this was like hearing God speak from a burning bush. It was the assurance they needed that He was there . . . and He was not silent.

Nancy's biggest frustration afterward was in dealing with insurance companies and trying to assess their material losses. Many possessions, of course, were irreplaceable personal items such as photographs and things handed down from parents and grandparents. But Nancy's highest priorities were her own two children, Joel and Holly, along with Jeff and Katie. The loss was hardest on them. Nancy said,

> They don't have the history of God's
> faithfulness that Ed and I have. We've
> had years to make deposits in our
> "faith account," but they haven't. We've
> learned that if you fail to stock up on
> faith when you don't need it, you won't
> have any when you do need it. This has
> been our opportunity to use what we've
> been learning.

While the world might view this as a senseless tragedy, deserving of resentment, Nancy and Ed saw God reveal Himself to them and refine them through this fire as He poured out a full measure of grace and peace.[7]

Suffering comes in many forms and degrees, but His grace is always there to carry us beyond it. I've lived long enough and endured a sufficient number of trials to say without hesitation that only our having Christ's perspective can replace our resentment with rejoicing. Jesus is the central piece of suffering's puzzle. If we fit Him into place, the rest of the puzzle—no matter how complex and enigmatic—begins to make sense.

Only Christ's salvation can change us from spectators to participants in the unfolding drama of redemption. The scenes will be demanding. Some may be tragic. But only then will we understand the role that suffering plays in our lives.

Only then will we be able to tap into hope beyond suffering.

My Questions and Thoughts

Chapter 2

A Soul Drenched in Tears

You Are Here

It was a foggy evening when a young man—
who only hours before had received a telegram
congratulating him on the birth of his first child—rode
a plodding train south from Albany, New York, to New
York City. He was traveling in response to a second
telegram, stating he must come home as quickly as
possible because his mother and his wife were both
dying . . . in the same house. Arriving at Grand Central
Station at 10:30 on the evening of February 13, 1884,
the young New York assemblyman made his way
through the fog-clouded streets to his home on West
Fifty-seventh Street. Earlier in the day, his brother had
told their sister, "There is a curse on this house. Mother
is dying, and Alice is dying too." [1]

The house was as dark as his brother's pronounce-
ment. A single gaslight flickered on the third floor.
The young man rushed up the stairs and found his
wife semi-comatose. Taking her in his arms he held
her, listening to the midnight bell toll on Fifth Avenue,
announcing the arrival of St. Valentine's Day. At two
in the morning, a message came from downstairs: if
he wanted to see his mother before she died he must
come now. At three, his mother slipped away, the result

of acute typhoid fever. Looking down at her peaceful but lifeless face he repeated his brother's proclamation: "There is a curse on this house."[2]

Bewildered and heartsick, he climbed back up the stairs and took his wife in his arms once again. Throughout the wee hours of the morning, he willed life into his beloved, but by two that afternoon, Alice Lee died of Bright's disease. That evening, on February 14, 1884, this young man and brand-new father drew a large cross in his diary and wrote beneath it: "The light has gone out of my life."[3]

On that darkest of days, that day of love and love lost, it certainly seemed that the light of his life had been blown out by the ice-cold wind of sudden death. Yet this young man would later become a hero of the Spanish-American War and then serve as governor of New York, vice president of the United States, and eventually as president. Besides the daughter he had with Alice Lee, he would father five more children with his second wife, Edith. And few men have ever grinned larger or longer, laughed more heartily, or had a greater lust for life than Theodore Roosevelt.

 ## Discovering the Way

Though the light of Roosevelt's life hadn't been completely snuffed out, stories like his remind us that a single moment in time can change a life forever. In that split second, when life is no longer what it once was, suffering, in all its brutality, wrenches our souls. In the depths of pain, we tend to ask five key questions: Why me? How long? What if . . . ? Where's God? How do I endure?

Recount a time in your life when you felt like the light had gone out of your life.

_____

_____

_____

_____

_____

_____

What questions did you ask?

_____

_____

_____

_____

_____

_____

What answers did you receive?

_____

_____

_____

_____

_____

_____

Why Me?

In the midst of suffering, our minds are as restless as our souls are inconsolable. And though God's answer to suffering is the empty cross and the empty grave of Christ, which does provide tremendous hope, the reality remains: neither the cross nor the tomb nor Christ Himself removes affliction from our lives. Agonies still seem unbearable, and a cry is wrung from our hearts like water from a wet rag: *"Why me?"*

Suffering always catches us by surprise — in the blink of an eye, our world changes, either for a moment (a stubbed toe) or for a lifetime (the death of a spouse or of a child). N. T. Wright was correct: "We ignore [suffering] when it doesn't hit us in the face, [and] we are surprised by [suffering] when it does." [4]

Friedrich Nietzsche said that "if you have your *why* for life, you can get by with almost any *how*." [5] But if we had answers to all of our "whys," would it make much difference? Answers offer some hope, but they don't deaden the reality of the pain that has overtaken our lives. Would Job have received much consolation in knowing that God was gambling with Job's integrity (Job 1:1–12; 2:1–6)? Such knowledge clearly wouldn't have brought his children or his health back (1:18–19; 2:7–8). God deemed it best not to answer Job's questions but to provide what Job really needed — the awesome reality and presence of the omniscient One (38:1–41:34).

We ask the question, "Why me?" because we have succumbed to the influence of a self-consumed society that teaches us to believe we can and should escape suffering. When suffering comes, we are caught off

guard and feel the violation as deeply personal, but this
was not so with Job. When calamity came upon Job,
he didn't invite it, but neither was he surprised: "The
LORD gave and the LORD has taken away. . . . Shall we
indeed accept good from God and not accept adversity?"
(Job 1:21; 2:10).

$\mathcal{H}$ow $\mathcal{L}$ong?

Following closely behind "Why me?"—even in the same
breath—we want to know when the sharp knife of pain
will be removed. The unknown reserves for sufferers
a special agony—the slow turning of the clock and
calendar and the haunting question: *"How long?"*

**Read the following passages. What question is asked
in each? What circumstances prompted each question?**

Psalm 13:1–2

_____

_____

_____

_____

Habakkuk 1:2–4

_____

_____

_____

_____

Revelation 6:9–10

_____

_____

_____

What If?

When we're enduring suffering, perhaps the most destructive question we ask is, "*What if?*" "What if the guy hadn't gone to the bar and then driven drunk?" "What if he had stayed at the bar and had two more drinks?" "What if I had left home earlier, or later, or not at all?" "What if . . ?" This question can stalk us, and in this way it is sadistic because it is unanswerable. We cannot change history, yet this question toys with the soul, convincing us to believe in the phantom hope that history can be reversed, that the waters under the bridge can be rolled back.

Have you ever been tortured by the "what if" question? If so, describe that experience.

_____

_____

_____

_____

_____

_____

Where's God?

Those caught in the swirl of suffering feel as if they have been dumped into hell's inner circle, where the gate reads: "Abandon every hope, who enter here."[6] Such hopelessness and isolation prompted Simone Weil to write:

> Affliction is anonymous . . . it deprives
> its victims of their personality and makes
> them into things. It is indifferent; and it

is the coldness of this indifference—a
metallic coldness—that freezes all those
it touches right to the depths of their
souls. They will never find warmth
again. They will never believe any more
that they are anyone.[7]

When suffering, as Weil described, washes over us
like a tidal wave, we gasp, *"Where's God?"*

**We think of Job as the great questioner in the midst
of suffering. He wasn't; he was only the most well
known. The greatest questioner was God Himself.
What was Jesus's cry on the cross, according to
Matthew 27:46?**

_____

_____

_____

_____

**What hope or comfort might Jesus's question give
you in the midst of your suffering?**

_____

_____

_____

_____

Starting Your Journey

It is God's presence that we most need in our
affliction. But often it is His presence that
seems most conspicuously absent at these times. Such
was the case for C. S. Lewis when he sat down after the
death of his wife, Joy, and with raw emotion penned
these words:

Where is God? This is one of the most disquieting symptoms. When you are happy, so happy that you have no sense of needing Him, so happy that you are tempted to feel His claims upon you as an interruption, if you remember yourself and turn to Him with gratitude and praise, you will be — or so it feels — welcomed with open arms. But go to Him when your need is desperate, when all other help is vain, and what do you find? A door slammed in your face, and a sound of bolting and double bolting on the inside. After that, silence. You may as well turn away. The longer you wait, the more emphatic the silence will become. There are no lights in the windows. It might be an empty house. Was it ever inhabited? It seemed so once. And that seeming was as strong as this. What can this mean? Why is He so present a commander in our time of prosperity and so very absent a help in time of trouble?[8]

Trying to kick down heaven's door will not budge it one bit. Nor will turning away. A shaken fist at God cannot be filled. Neither helps you endure affliction. We must come to God gently tapping, waiting with open hands, and then by His grace we'll eventually see the door open and read the banner announcing His help: *J-E-S-U-S L-O-V-E-S YOU.*

How Do I Endure?

We've looked at four of the five key questions we frequently ask when experiencing pain and suffering. To answer the fifth question, *"How do I endure?"* the Bible affirms five profound principles, which we've spelled out using the letters "J-E-S-U-S." The Bible also advises obedience to five practical practices to help us endure, which we've spelled out using the letters "L-O-V-E-S."

We should affirm five profound principles when we suffer: J-E-S-U-S.

Jesus will never abandon us. No matter how abandoned we feel or how many doors seem to slam in our faces, Jesus will never, ever abandon us. Greek scholar Kenneth Wuest captured the passion of Hebrews 13:5 when he translated the Lord's affirmation: "I will not, I will not cease to sustain and uphold you. I will not, I will not, I will not let you down." [9]

Every tear will be wiped away. No tear that drops from our eyes will ever be in vain. God will see to that.

What truth about God is found in each of the following passages?

Psalm 56:8

_____

_____

_____

_____

Revelation 21:4

_____

_____

_____

_____

What hope do these promises give you in the midst of suffering?

_____

_____

_____

_____

Signs of faith are held high when we ask questions. Questions are not necessarily signs of doubt; in fact, they may be signs of faith. When we ask questions in faith, we inherently reaffirm God's goodness and power because we recognize that things are out of joint — things are not the way they should be — and we are asking God to put things back into joint, to make things right.

Unseen and unheard, yet our God is trustworthy. Though we've not seen Him with our eyes and though we've not heard Him with our ears, He is our God, and we can trust Him — even in the midst of suffering.

What was Job's great hope in Job 23:8–10?

_____

_____

_____

_____

Do you believe this is true of you? Why, or why not?

_____

_____

_____

_____

Sorrow will turn into joy. On the day Jesus wipes away our tears and does away with mourning and death (Revelation 21:4), oh, the joy that shall flood our souls! "I'll convert their weeping into laughter," the Lord promised, "lavishing comfort, invading their grief with joy" (Jeremiah 31:13 MSG). What a day that will be!

We have learned five profound principles that we ought to remember and claim when we are afflicted:

> Jesus will never abandon us.
>
> Every tear will be wiped away.
>
> Signs of faith are held high when we ask questions.
>
> Unseen and unheard, yet our God is trustworthy.
>
> Sorrow will turn into joy.

We should perform five practical practices when we suffer: L-O-V-E-S.

Learn to forgive. Often our suffering is the result of nature or accidents, but many times we suffer as a result of someone else's or our own foolishness or lack of forethought. In either case, we must learn to forgive.

What is the principle Jesus laid down in
Matthew 18:21–22?

_____

_____

_____

_____

What is the principle Paul laid down in
Romans 12:19?

_____

_____

_____

_____

Is there someone you need to forgive? _____

Who? _____

Sometimes the path of forgiveness is long and
winding, and that's okay. It starts with a single step:
willingness. Will you ask God to move you closer to
the next step in your process? _____

Forgiveness and even reconciliation don't ensure an
end to painful circumstances, but obedience and letting
go of bitterness do open the door to inner peace and
freedom.

Observe and hold on to simple truths and practices.
As hard as it is to pray when we suffer, we must. If we
can't form the words of a prayer, then we can pray the
Psalms or pray the book of Lamentations. After we
pray, we praise. David, when he cried out, "How long,
O LORD?" also sang to the Lord for His gracious bounty
(Psalm 13:1, 6). Praise lifts our eyes from ourselves up to

God. Next, we can claim the promises of God. In your suffering, turn to God's promises in Scripture, and you'll find courage and healing for your soul. It's in the Word that you'll discover old and simple truths that bring comfort.

What promises are found in these passages? Summarize each in your own words.

Matthew 6:34

_____

_____

_____

_____

John 11:25

_____

_____

_____

_____

What other promises from the Scripture can you hold on to during times of suffering?

_____

_____

_____

_____

_____

Vent our emotions. Jesus was the supreme example of balance (John 11:33–38). When Lazarus, Jesus's friend whom He loved dearly, died, Jesus wept openly and freely. He held nothing back. He also expressed

His raging anger, not at God but at death itself. When John recorded that Jesus was "deeply moved," John used a verb that expresses fury and outrage. The Greek playwright Aeschylus used the same verb to describe warhorses raring up on hind legs and snorting out of their nostrils before charging into battle.

Venting your emotions appropriately—not shaking a fist at God or cursing Him for the trouble in your life—will keep you from becoming bitter or sliding into the pit of depression. You can express emotions to God through prayer or confide in a close Christian friend or counselor. Be sure to choose someone who is safe, who will keep confidences, who will listen with empathy, and who will speak the truth in love.

Eat, dress, and sleep. Can it get more basic than this? Often when our bodies and souls have been shocked into the reality of suffering, we neglect our physical needs.

Read Acts 27:33–36. Describe the circumstances and the emotional climate at the time (see also verse 20). What did Paul encourage the sailors to do? And what was the response?

_____

_____

_____

_____

_____

_____

_____

_____

_____

Read 2 Timothy 4:13. What did Paul ask for? Why do you think Paul wanted these particular items as he sat in prison knowing he would die soon?

_____

_____

_____

_____

_____

_____

_____

Why do you think it's so hard for us to prioritize our own physical care when we're in a crisis? What are some practical ways to avoid this pitfall?

_____

_____

_____

_____

_____

_____

_____

Taking care of ourselves doesn't deny the reality of anguish, but it does affirm life.

Share our suffering with others. We must force ourselves to reach out. Ask for help. No one is so big that he
or she doesn't need others. John Donne famously wrote,

> No man is an island, entire of itself;
> every man is a piece of the continent,
> a part of the main. If a clod be washed
> away by the sea, Europe is the less . . .
> any man's death diminishes me, because
> I am involved in mankind, and therefore
> never send to know for whom the bell
> tolls; it tolls for thee.[10]

Slow, agonizing soul-death comes from isolation.
But life and health spring anew in community. Paul
understood this and rallied his friends around him
at his most agonizing moments. With emotion and
urgency, Paul wrote to Timothy: "Make every effort to
come to me soon. . . . Only Luke is with me. Pick up
Mark and bring him with you, for he is useful to me for
service. . . . Make every effort to come before winter"
(2 Timothy 4:9, 11, 21).

Solomon said that "a cord of three strands is not
quickly torn apart" (Ecclesiastes 4:12). In our pain we
don't have to retreat into a shell of sorrow. We can call
for help and ask friends to come quickly.

Who can you call on when you face suffering?

_____

_____

_____

_____

Again, here are five practical practices we ought to perform when we are afflicted:

Learn to forgive.

Observe and hold on to simple truths and practices.

Vent our emotions.

Eat, dress, and sleep.

Share our suffering with others.

The wonderful but little-known movie *Wit* contains a scene that subtly communicates the truth that Jesus is with us in our suffering. Emma Thompson's character, Vivian Bearing, is a brilliant professor of English literature, specializing in the holy sonnets of John Donne. With biting wit, she educates her students, but she also alienates them. After being diagnosed with cancer, she undergoes eight months of severe and experimental treatments. Single and friendless, the teacher becomes a subject for student doctors, a specimen for probing eyes and poking hands.

Toward the end of the movie, when it is clear that the agony of the chemotherapy treatments will not stave off the agony of the cancer, Vivian has a visitor—her first. It is her mentor, another brilliant John Donne scholar. She comforts Vivian, not with a poem by Donne, but with a children's book by Margaret Wise Brown, *The Runaway Bunny.* The simple lesson of the story, which Vivian's mentor called a "little allegory of the soul," is: "Wherever [the soul] hides, God will find it." [11]

Our souls tend to retreat when we suffer. But wherever they retreat to, God is there. Jesus loves you—you do not suffer alone.

My Questions and Thoughts

Chapter 3

What Job Teaches Us about Ourselves

Children have a way of saying things that often make us smile. They don't mean to be funny, but more often than not, they are. This usually happens when they're answering questions—serious questions. As they give their opinions, we can't help but laugh.

Take for example the subject of love and marriage:

- "How do you decide who to marry?"
  Kirsten, age 10: "No person really decides before they grow up who they're going to marry. God decides it all way before, and you get to find out later who you're stuck with."

- "How can a stranger tell if two people are married?"
  Derrick, age 8: "You might have to guess, like maybe if they were yelling at the same kids."

- "What do you think your mom and dad have in common?"
  Lori, age 8: "Both don't want any more kids."

- "When is it okay to kiss someone?"
  Pam, age 7: "When they're rich."

- "Is it better to be single or married?"
  Anita, age 9: "It's better for girls to be single but not for boys. Boys need someone to clean up after them."

- "How would you make a marriage work?"
  Ricky, age 10: "Tell your wife that she looks pretty even if she looks like a truck." [1]

Some of the notes that have been handed (or e-mailed) to me about my sermons on Job have been hilarious! One child asked her daddy if their pastor's name was now Job. Another 10-year-old kept giving me pictures he had drawn depicting the scenes I described in one sermon after another. (You should see some of those boils!) Finally, as I got near the end of the book, he stopped drawing. No more pictures, but I did get a small two-sentence note, which read, "Can you find another subject? I've run out of ideas." Gotta love that honesty.

Job is a long and challenging book, and if you ever read or study it, you'll come to know two things for sure: first, Job isn't shallow entertainment, an easy story to stay interested in; second, there's a reason there aren't many books written on Job.

It may not be very exciting, and it certainly isn't a simple plot to unravel, but what Job lacks in popular appeal he makes up for in realism. The long hallways of a leukemia ward in a hospital may not be exciting or creative, but each room contains people asking the same questions and wrestling with the same issues as Job. Exciting and entertaining it isn't but substantive and real? In spades!

What happens in places like that and in books like this is that you find yourself paying less attention to the temporal and the externals. You give increasingly more attention to the internal and the eternal. To what is going on deep within.

Soul-searching replaces channel surfing. You start asking questions that are hard to answer. You think a lot deeper about the things all of this is teaching you. What does Job teach us about ourselves?

My primary goal in this chapter may surprise you. It is neither to inform nor reprove. And I certainly don't need to repeat the details of Job's story. My goal is to intensify your enthusiasm for life—to move you from a day-by-day toleration of the status-quo mentality to a renewal of your drive to really come alive. The word is *passion*.

Benjamin Zander, professor at the New England Conservatory of Music, illustrated what I'm hoping to accomplish.

> A young pianist was playing a Chopin prelude in my master class, and although we had worked right up to the edge of realizing an overarching concept of the piece, his performance remained earthbound. He understood it intellectually, he could have explained it to someone else, but he was unable to convey the emotional energy that is the true language of music. Then I noticed something that proved to be the key: His body was firmly centered in the upright position. I blurted out, "The trouble is you're a two-buttock player!" I encouraged him to allow his whole body to flow sideways, urging him to catch the wave of the music with the

shape of his own body, and suddenly the music took flight. Several in the audience gasped, feeling the emotional dart hit home, as a new distinction was born: the *one-buttock* player. The president of a corporation in Ohio, who was present as a witness, wrote to me: "I was so moved that I went home and transformed my whole company into a *one-buttock* company."

I never did find out what he meant by that, but I have my own ideas. . . .

I met Jacqueline Du Pre in the 1950s, when I was twenty and she was fifteen, a gawky English schoolgirl who blossomed into the greatest cellist of her generation. We performed the Two Cello Quintet of Schubert together, and I remember her playing was like a tidal wave of intensity and passion. When she was six years old, the story goes, she went into her first competition as a cellist, and she was seen running down the corridor carrying her cello above her head, with a huge grin of excitement on her face. A custodian, noting what he took to be relief on the little girl's face, said, "I see you've just had your chance to play!" And Jackie answered, excitedly, "No, no, I'm just about to!"

Even at six, Jackie was a conduit for music to pour through.[2]

Put bluntly, my hope is to help you become a "one-buttock player" on life's keyboard, not satisfied with pounding out another year of dull, predictable notes and chords but throwing yourself full-bore into the symphony!

Seven Lessons Worth Remembering

> There was a man in the land of Uz
> whose name was Job; and that man was
> blameless, upright, fearing God and
> turning away from evil. (Job 1:1)

We soon discover Job and his wife had seven sons and three daughters. His possessions were great, with thousands of sheep and camels, along with half a thousand oxen and donkeys. In fact, the word was out on this man: he was "the greatest of all the men of the east" (Job 1:3). There was no one better known and probably no one wealthier. Job had it made.

Without his knowing it, a dialogue took place in the invisible world above. As the Lord and Satan had their strange encounter, the subject quickly turned to this well-known earthly individual. The Lord called Satan's attention to Job's exemplary life, and Satan responded with a sinister sneer. "Of course, who wouldn't serve You the way You've prospered and protected him. Take away all the perks and watch what happens; the man will turn on You in a flash." God agreed to let the Adversary unload on Job.

And so, in today's terms, the Lord bet Satan that Job would never turn away. We could refer to that agreement as the "divine wager." Satan then instigated a sudden and hostile removal of all Job's possessions, leaving him bankrupt. Within a matter of minutes, everything he owned was gone.

This brings us to the first of seven lessons worth remembering: *we never know ahead of time the plans God has for us.* Job had no prior knowledge or warning. That morning dawned like every other morning. The night had passed like any other night. There was no great angelic manifestation—not even a tap on his window or a note left on the kitchen table.

In one calamity after another, all the buildings on his land were gone, and nothing but lumber and bodies littered the landscape. It occurred so fast, Job's mind swirled in disbelief. Everything hit broadside . . . his world instantly changed.

You and I must learn from this! We never know what a day will bring, good or ill. Our heavenly Father's plan unfolds apart from our awareness. Ours is a walk of faith, not sight. Trust, not touch. Leaning long and hard, not running away. No one knows ahead of time what the Father's plan includes. It's best that way. It may be a treasured blessing; it could be a test that drops us to our knees. He knows ahead of time, but He is not obligated to warn us about it or to remind us it's on the horizon. We can be certain of this: our God knows what is best.

Read the following Scriptures slowly and thoughtfully:

> I know, O LORD, that a man's way is not
>   in himself,
> Nor is it in a man who walks to direct
>   his steps.
> Correct me, O LORD, but with justice;
> Not with Your anger, or You will bring
>   me to nothing. (Jeremiah 10:23–24)

"For I know the plans that I have for you," declares the LORD, "plans for welfare and not for calamity to give you a future and a hope. Then you will call upon Me and come and pray to Me, and I will listen to you. You will seek Me and find Me when you search for Me with all your heart." (Jeremiah 29:11–13)

The mind of man plans his way,
But the LORD directs his steps.
(Proverbs 16:9)

Man's steps are ordained by the LORD,
How then can man understand his way?
(20:24)

"For My thoughts are not your thoughts,
Nor are your ways My ways," declares
        the LORD.
"For as the heavens are higher than the
        earth,
So are My ways higher than your ways
And My thoughts than your thoughts."
(Isaiah 55:8–9)

Be anxious for nothing, but in everything by prayer and supplication with thanksgiving let your requests be made known to God. And the peace of God, which surpasses all comprehension, will guard your hearts and your minds in Christ Jesus. (Philippians 4:6–7)

Consider it all joy, my brethren, when
you encounter various trials, knowing
that the testing of your faith produces
endurance. And let endurance have
its perfect result, so that you may be
perfect and complete, lacking in
nothing. (James 1:2–4)

Therefore humble yourselves under
the mighty hand of God, that He may
exalt you at the proper time, casting all
your anxiety on Him, because He cares
for you. (1 Peter 5:6–7)

Did you do as I asked? Did you read each one slowly
and thoughtfully?

The ultimate plan our Lord has for us is not a
calamitous, fatalistic, heartbreaking, life-ending set of
events, designed to weaken and destroy our faith. On
the contrary, it is a plan that is for our "welfare" to give
us "a future and a hope," wrote the prophet Jeremiah.
But that doesn't mean it will be easy or comfortable.
Because He is a God of the unexpected, it will be
surprising! It will be different than you or I would have
ever pondered or planned or, for that matter, preferred.
Therefore, to increase your passion for life, I have some
pretty simple advice: be ready for anything. And I do
mean anything.

One of my friends at our church told me that one
of his longtime friends who had a well-paying job
got notice from the National Guard that he was being
called up. No heads-up warning. This meant an
immediate change of lifestyle. He had to leave his
excellent occupation in order to serve in the Guard.
He and his wife (and several kids) needed to sell their

lovely home. She was forced to adjust to a completely different world without the constant companionship and support of her husband. They did not know where they would live, what schools the children would be attending, or how safe he'd be during his tour of military duty. It came like a bolt out of the blue.

We have no guarantee that life will rock along for us as it has this past year. What you enjoy today as a result of your good job and great health, you may not be enjoying this time next year or six months from now. This truth isn't designed to frighten you; it's designed to help prepare you for a whole new way of thinking. Our times are in His hands. Have you ever meditated on that thought; I mean really believed it?

Job's response, you will recall, is absolutely remarkable.

> Then Job arose and tore his robe and
> shaved his head, and he fell to the
> ground and worshiped. He said,
> "Naked I came from my mother's womb,
> And naked I shall return there.
> The LORD gave and the LORD has
>   taken away.
> Blessed be the name of the LORD."
> (Job 1:20–22)

Here's a second lesson worth remembering: *a vertical perspective will keep us from horizontal panic.* Don't misunderstand Job's response to the devastation. Job didn't escape into some mental state of denial. He faced the music—somber and sad that it was. He was so overwhelmed by all the loss, he tore his robe. He was broken and saddened and grieved over the death of his kids. That's why he shaved his head and later sat in ashes. In fact, these reactions assure us that he refused to escape emotionally through denial. But don't miss his ultimate response. He fell to the ground and worshiped.

His vertical perspective was clear and his will undaunted. Nothing that happened on the horizontal plane caused this man to panic. It's as if Job was saying, "I had. I enjoyed. I was blessed. I'm now without those benefits. They're no longer a part of my world. I'm heartbroken over the loss of my family. But the same God who gave all of this by His grace is the God who in His sovereign will has chosen to take it all away. I honor and praise Him. May His name be forever exalted!"

Francis Andersen's words are worth remembering.

> Job finds nothing wrong with what has happened to him. At this point Job's trial enters a new phase, the most trying of all. . . . He never curses God, but all his human relationships are broken. His attitude is the same as before (1:21). It is equally right for God to give gifts and to retrieve them . . . it is equally right for God to send *good* or *evil*. . . . Such positive faith is the magic stone that transmutes all to gold; for when the bad as well as the good is received *at the hand of God*, every experience of life becomes an occasion of blessing. But the cost is high. It is easier to lower your view of God than to raise your faith to such a height. [3]

When life trucks along comfortably and contentedly, in good health and with a happy family . . . my, my! How high our view of God can be! How thrilled we are with all those wonderful verses of Scripture. How we hang on the words of the pastor's sermons. And how fervently we sing the songs of celebration. But let hardship arrive or let our health take a nosedive, how quickly our song is silenced, how cynical our attitude, how sour our faith becomes, and how quickly we're tempted to lower our view of God. Andersen is correct. It's easy to question God when hard times replace good times. A strong vertical perspective fans the flame of passion.

Job had maintained his strong vertical perspective, though he had lost virtually everything. Job did not sin or blame God, which frustrated Satan but did not surprise our God. He knew Job would continue in his integrity. But the worst was yet to come.

As the next day dawned, Satan came out swinging. The Lord asked, "Have you noticed my servant, Job?" (Job 2:3). It must have been a great moment when the Lord could point to Job who had demonstrated no break in his faith, no doubt in his trust, and Satan had to face the music. Yet, refusing to accept defeat, the Accuser flashed that cynical sneer once again:

> Satan answered the LORD and said, "Skin for skin! Yes, all that a man has he will give for his life. However, put forth Your hand now, and touch his bone and his flesh; he will curse You to Your face." So the LORD said to Satan, "Behold, he is in your power, only spare his life." (Job 2:4 – 6)

You know all too well what happened. As soon as he got the green light:

> Satan went out from the presence of the
> Lord and smote Job with sore boils from
> the sole of his foot to the crown of his
> head. (Job 2:7)

Job was leveled to the ground, literally. His pain was beyond description. His fever was raging. He couldn't eat, couldn't sleep, and there was no sign of relief. His misery knew no bounds. Watching him suffer was more than his wife could endure. Seeing him sitting there in the ash heap, she could stay quiet no longer. She allowed herself to say the unthinkable.

> Do you still hold fast your integrity?
> Curse God and die! (Job 2:9)

She loved him; never doubt it. The sickness hadn't made her love him less. Her compassion overran her better judgment, and in that unguarded moment, she gave herself the freedom to verbalize an alien thought: "If you will curse God, He will take you on home. You and I both know this act will swiftly end the suffering." (Can you imagine the breathless anticipation of Satan at this moment?) Job may have been in misery, but he had enough presence of mind to detect heresy when he heard it.

> But he said to her, "You speak as one
> of the foolish women speaks. Shall we
> indeed accept good from God and not
> accept adversity?" (Job 2:10)

That statement provides us with a third lesson: *discernment. Discernment is needed to detect wrong advice from well-meaning people.* Those words whispered in his ear came from his wife! She'd loved him through ten births. She'd loved him through the rearing of all their children. She'd loved him from the lean, early days in business through the years of great prosperity where they could at last enjoy some relief. This woman loved him when he was a nobody, and she continued to love him when he became a household word in every home of the east. Job had known her love through all the years, but that had not blinded him from realizing her counsel was wrong. In effect, he thought, "Though spoken by one who loves me and wants what is best for me, I dare not heed her advice."

Consider her counsel long enough to understand how far off she was. She was questioning what God had admired, and she was encouraging what Satan had predicted. Think about it. God had said to Satan, "He still holds fast his integrity." And she was suggesting, "Job, no longer sustain your integrity."

Satan had said, "He will curse You to Your face." And she said to the man she loved, "Job, just curse God."

The Devil was on tiptoe, urging, "Yes! Yes! Do it!" And you know his demons were at work trying fervently to weaken Job. But Job stood firm. He discerned the error and flat-out rejected it.

Job knew he could not, in good faith, follow her advice, no matter how well-meaning she was. His response revealed his inner discipline. His words were bold and blunt:

> He told her, "You're talking like an empty-headed fool. We take the good days from God — why not also the bad days?" (Job 2:10 MSG)

What great theology! "God isn't our God only when times are good. Our faith in Him isn't limited to those days He blesses us. We don't claim Him as our Lord only when we get what we want. He's our God even when adversity strikes. He is Lord of good days and bad days. He didn't leave us the day we started suffering!" Job was right on. Talk about passion!

Consider a fourth lesson: *when things turn from bad to worse, sound theology helps us remain strong and stable.* It is a sign of maturity that Job, after suffering such a barrage of cataclysmic events, was thinking so clearly, so correctly without wavering. No uncertainty. The man did not entertain his wife's suggestion for a moment. "You speak as a fool," was his immediate reaction. "Surely you know by now these lips cannot curse God. Death is in His hands, not mine. When He's ready to take me, He'll take me." How could Job just give up on life? He was grounded in his knowledge of God. In times like that, sound theology is invaluable.

Reminds me of one of Charles Schultz's cartoons that I saw several years ago. Remember *Peanuts*? Linus with his blanket is standing at the picture window in the family room. Standing beside him is Lucy, who, of course, is in charge. They're watching it rain, and it is coming down in sheets. They can hardly see the trees in the backyard. Lucy sighs, "Boy, look at all that rain. What if it floods the whole world?" Linus answers without hesitation, "It will never do that. In the ninth chapter of Genesis, God promised Noah that would never happen again. And the sign of the promise is the rainbow." Lucy looks at him, shakes her head and says, "You've taken a great load off my mind." He responds immediately, "Sound theology has a way of doing that!" [4]

Maybe her husband's retort took a big load off Mrs. Job's mind. How memorable it is when the one who is suffering can teach the one who is well. Sound theology provides a foundation like nothing else. Quick reminder here: be careful that you never substitute psychological gobbledygook for good biblical theology. Work hard at not weakening your theological foundation by double talk. Don't go there. It will backfire on you when you least expect it.

On my birthday, I got one of my favorite kind of greeting cards—one of those funny cards. There's a guy hanging by his collar on the limb of a tree. His feet and legs are dangling about two feet off the ground. He's limp and helpless, as his camera hangs loosely from his neck. Two huge bears are off to the side discussing his fate. One bear says to the other, "His name's Bradshaw. He says he understands I came from a single parent den with inadequate role models. He senses that my dysfunctional behavior is shame-based and codependent and he urges me to let my inner cub heal." A little pause for thought, then he concludes: "I say we eat him."

Stick with sound theology. Steer clear of pop psychology with its confusing nomenclature. It seems reasonable at the moment, but when you need something of substance, it will neither stabilize nor strengthen you. A life of passionate enthusiasm needs to stay grounded on granite-like theological truth.

Finally, Job's friends showed up. That was when things turned south. But you wouldn't know that right away. At first they seemed like reasonable and caring men.

> Now when Job's three friends heard of
> all this adversity that had come upon
> him, they came each one from his own
> place, Eliphaz the Temanite, Bildad the

Shuhite and Zophar the Naamathite;
and they made an appointment together
to come to sympathize with him and
comfort him. When they lifted up their
eyes at a distance and did not recognize
him, they raised their voices and wept.
And each of them tore his robe and they
threw dust over their heads toward the
sky. Then they sat down on the ground
with him for seven days and seven
nights with no one speaking a word to
him, for they saw that his pain was very
great. (Job 2:11–13)

This introduces us to a fifth lesson worth remembering: *caring and sensitive friends know when to come, how to respond, and what to say.* I so wish that Eliphaz, Bildad, and Zophar had simply stayed silent, remained near to comfort Job and his wife, brought a bowl of soup or broth and a cool cup of water when needed. These men qualified on the first two, didn't they? They knew when to come to Job. Soon as they got word of his devastating circumstances, they dropped everything and came to his side. And at least initially (for seven days), they responded the right way. They simply sat alongside. No doubt they hurt for him, prayed for the man and his wife, and hoped to sympathize and comfort.

We who have been hospitalized know the joy of looking across the room and seeing the faces of a couple or three friends. What comfort to know they cared enough to be near. Down deep inside, we're grateful they're not saying much. They're not in our face "preaching" to us or trying to explain why we're suffering. They're just staying near. Love brought them, compassion flows from them, and gentleness draws us to them.

But the wheels started coming off the cart when those same men broke the silence. They felt the need to open Job's eyes and spell out the reasons for his afflictions. Perhaps they meant well when they started, but their "good advice" quickly eroded. They rebuked him. They questioned his motives. They probed ever deeper for hidden, secret sins. The damage they did was unconscionable.

All of us who desire to live life with passion need to spend some time evaluating our compassion. You and I will sometimes find ourselves in the role of a caring friend, hopefully a sensitive friend. Everyone who is hurting needs a friend—a friend outside the family. They don't need many, only a few faithful friends. These are the ones who bring comfort and a sensitive spirit to the hurting. They are rare, and their reassuring presence is invaluable. We need friends who love us genuinely and, on occasion, friends who confront us wisely.

David comes to mind. Early on, not long after being anointed as the future king of Israel, the young giant-killer found himself hunted and haunted by King Saul who became insanely jealous of him. Saul's son, Jonathan, heard the inappropriate comments his father made about David. Jonathan knew that they were inaccurate, prejudiced, and extreme. He sensed real trouble brewing in his father's heart. Overnight, Jonathan took up the cause of David and became David's closest friend. He sought David out wherever he was hiding. He wouldn't let David suffer alone. He listened. He reassured. He understood. He offered words of hope and encouragement. That's the role Jonathan filled. "He loved him as he loved his own life" (1 Samuel 20:17).

As time passed, both Saul and Jonathan died violent, tragic deaths. David became the king, and many years later, he plunged into a snake pit of carnality, adultery, murder, and shameless hypocrisy. Not surprisingly, this took a terrible toll on his leadership. Out of the shadows emerged another faithful friend, Nathan, who was equally sensitive and caring. Nathan's role was different from Jonathan's. Nathan was used by the Lord to confront his friend and to help restore his integrity. Nathan arrested David's attention and turned his heart back to God in true repentance. Everyone needs a Jonathan. Everyone needs a Nathan. Whichever role we play, it's important to remain caring and sensitive. To know when to come, to know how to respond, and to know what to say when we speak.

Overwhelmed by his situation, Job ultimately let it all out. He could hold it in no longer. He opened his mouth with outbursts of frustration. He cursed the day he was born. He even went back nine months earlier than that and despised the moment he was conceived. Everything poured out in a stream of excessive words.

> "Let the day perish on which I was to
>   be born,
> And the night which said, 'A boy is
>   conceived.'
> May that day be darkness;
> Let not God above care for it,
> Nor light shine on it.
> Let darkness and black gloom claim it;
> Let a cloud settle on it;
> Let the blackness of the day terrify it."
> (Job 3:3–5)

He then cursed the fact he didn't die at birth.

> "Why did I not die at birth,
> Come forth from the womb and expire?
> Why did the knees receive me,
> And why the breasts, that I should suck?
> For now I would have lain down and
> been quiet;
> I would have slept then, I would have
> been at rest." (Job 3:11–13)

With that, he dumped out the rest of his frustration:

> "For what I fear comes upon me,
> And what I dread befalls me.
> I am not at ease, nor am I quiet,
> And I am not at rest, but turmoil
> comes." (Job 3:25–26)

Those are the exclamations of a man who had come to his wits' end: he'd lost everything. His health was now gone, bringing indescribable pain, and the suffering didn't end. The kids were still dead. There was not enough money to provide for what was needed. His surroundings were atrocious. His wife was there, albeit disillusioned, urging him to pack it in. *That was enough!* Even a man of integrity has his limits. Job must have finished his verbal eruption with his head in his hands, heaving audible sobs.

That's when the friends turned to vultures and began their feeding frenzy. Such inappropriate reactions provide us with a sixth lesson: *it's easy to be Monday-morning quarterbacks when we encounter another's outburst.* Admittedly, it is not easy to hear the kind of things Job blurted out. Not being in his place, not feeling his pain, not knowing his thoughts or his fears—not really—it is the most natural response imaginable to react:

> "I would never say that—and he
>   shouldn't!"
> "I would never do what he's done—
>   and he shouldn't!"
> "I would always say and do
>   this—and he should!"

And all of that leads to, "Job, don't say that. You are really going to regret it!" But the fact is he was the one going through it. He was the one in the heat of the battle. He was there; they were not. They just thought they knew what they'd say or do.

Monday-morning quarterbacks think, *I would never react like that. I would never say such a thing to God.* And then the clincher: *This is how I would respond. I mean, how could she call herself a Christian and act like that? Why, if I were the Lord, I'd discipline her for that.*

Monday-morning quarterbacks are notorious for knowing everything! And pointing out every mistake. (We don't even wait until Monday morning!) "Don't throw that pass, you idiot!" "They've got the split end covered!" "They're gonna intercept if you throw it—don't!" (Interception.) "No!" "When are you gonna get a life?" we yell at the game on television. And most of us have never been quarterbacks. We've certainly never had three or four six-foot-nine-inch, 370-pound linemen with blood in their eyes and fangs sticking out of their lips running full speed in our direction—grinning. And we say, "Don't throw that thing, you dodo! Don't throw it! If I were there, I wouldn't have thrown it. I'd take a hit."

Uh, yeah . . . sure.

Stop that nonsense. Let's agree to allow our Job-friend the space to unload without getting our lecture. It will help if we remember things we shouldn't have said. We, too, have said things that were wrong or inappropriate. We, too, have responded incorrectly when the heat was on. We, too, have run off at the mouth. We, too, have thrown verbal interceptions. When we did, we didn't need someone to tell us we blew it. Within seconds, we realized it. We may even think at the time we're doing it, *I'm gonna regret this*. But we still do it.

You'll need this lesson. You'll need this principle, especially if you're a spiritual leader, if you teach an adult Bible study, if you're a counselor at a church, or if you're a pastor on the staff. The world is too full of the dogmatic "I told you so" or "You really shouldn't" or "You ought to." Just be quiet. Pray silently. Try hard to imagine the pain.

Eliphaz landed on Job with both feet. Fists were swinging—round one, round two, round three—punching at Job. Then Bildad hit him. Then Zophar beat up on him. Not one of those guys had *ever* gone through anything like what Job was going through. So, they poured out all their "good advice." Friendships will not stand the strain of too much "good advice" for very long.

We hardly need to be reminded that Job ultimately saw the error of his way. And what did he do? He openly acknowledged it: "I retract, / And I repent" (Job 42:6). What a great man! He suffered through all of this for who knows how long. Weeks? Maybe months? Too long! Finally, after proving himself a man of heroic endurance, the Lord called Job His "servant" (four times). The Lord then rebuked the friends who had made such a mess of the situation.

> It came about after the LORD had spoken
> these words to Job, that the LORD said
> to Eliphaz the Temanite, "My wrath
> is kindled against you and against
> your two friends, because you have
> not spoken of Me what is right as My
> servant Job has." (Job 42:7)

The Lord abundantly rewarded His servant for his sustained integrity as well as his submissive spirit. But mainly, God honored Job because of his faithful endurance, which provides our seventh and final lesson worth remembering: *the cultivation of obedient endurance is the crowning mark of maturity.* A major goal of wholesome, healthy Christians is reaching maturity before death overtakes us. I will tell you without hesitation that one of my major goals in life is to grow up as I grow older. A commendable etching on a gravestone would be: "Here lies a man who kept growing as he kept aging." Growing up and growing old need to walk hand in hand. Never doubt it: maturing is a slow, arduous process. Job accomplished it; he reached that goal. Small wonder we read that he died an old man and full of days. He lived the rest of his years (140 more) full of enthusiasm and passion. What an enviable way to finish one's life.

When trouble comes, we have two options. We can view it as an intrusion, an outrage, or we can see it as an opportunity to respond in specific obedience to God's will. This is that rugged virtue James calls "endurance."

Endurance is not jaw-clenched resignation, nor is it passive acquiescence. It is "a long obedience in the same direction." It is staying on the path of obedience despite counterindications. It is a dogged determination to pursue holiness when the conditions of holiness are not favorable. It is a choice in the midst of our suffering to do what God has asked us to do, whatever it is, and for as long He asks us to do it. As Oswald Chambers wrote, "To choose to suffer means that there is something wrong; *to choose God's will even if it means suffering is a very different thing*" (emphasis added). [5]

What a Way to Go

Where are you today? Where is your journey leading you? More importantly, which option have you chosen? Are you viewing your trial as an outrage or an opportunity? Try hard not to forget the list of seven lessons Job teaches us about ourselves. Do you keep a journal? If you do, I've got a practical suggestion. Go back through this chapter and transfer the seven lessons onto a page of your journal. Think through your current situation and apply whichever ones are appropriate. Return to that page every month or so. It will make an enormous difference. As you grow older, you will keep growing up. And, instead of simply reading about the life of Job, you will begin living that kind of life.

That makes all the sense in the world.

My Questions and Thoughts

Chapter 4

A Deeper Mystery

You Are Here

If you were a Polish Jew living in Krakow in 1942, Oskar Schindler would have been one of the last men in Poland, or anywhere in Europe for that matter, to whom you'd have entrusted your life or the lives of your family. Schindler was a Nazi profiteer. If Hitler didn't succeed in keeping the war going, then Schindler didn't make money from war contracts. And Schindler liked to make money. He also liked to spend money.

Schindler spent millions of dollars keeping Jewish families together and protecting them from Hitler's gas chambers and ovens. At war's end he had spent everything he had in order to save 1,100 Jews. Why? Why would Schindler spend his entire fortune to save these few Jews from extermination? What did he care if 1,100 Jewish workers were liquidated? There were plenty of others who could take their places in his factory. Money was Schindler's goal and god. And yet, he made a list. "The list is life," Itzhak Stern told Schindler in the movie *Schindler's List*. "The list is an absolute good." [1]

It was. But where does such goodness come from?

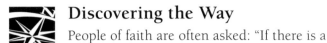

Discovering the Way

People of faith are often asked: "If there is a good God, why is there evil and suffering in the world?" Sometimes this is asked as a philosophical challenge to Christianity. In that case, another question must be asked in reply, a question for those outside the family of faith: "If there is no God, why is there goodness in the world?" What accounts for an Oskar Schindler?

But often the question of God's goodness and human suffering wells up from a suffering soul that cannot see beyond or comprehend its own pain. These dear folks are seeking relief. Our answers, however, will be little comfort if we do not first understand something about the mystery of goodness.

What would you say accounts for goodness in the world?

_____

_____

_____

_____

_____

_____

A Deeper Mystery

George Orwell observed, "Most people get a fair amount of fun out of their lives, but on balance life is suffering, and only the very young or the very foolish imagine otherwise."[2] Obviously, plenty of people are corrupt and corruptible, greedy and deceptive. And there is too much murder, rape, and warfare to go around. If we watch enough news, we'll get the impression that the world is all bad, all the time, all over the place. Like Chicken Little, we'll believe the sky is falling all around us—global warming, global terrorism, global pandemics, global economic collapse, unceasing warfare, and misery without end. But this is not so. Suffering may be taking place all the time somewhere in the world, but it isn't taking place in each and every place in the world all the time. Goodness is. Why?

Why, on the whole, is there more goodness in the world than evil?

As people of faith, we profess that God made the world good, that we made it bad, and that God will make it good again. Though there is much evil in the world, there is still much good in the world. In fact, in comparison to evil and suffering, goodness exceeds evil. And while tragedies certainly happen, most of us will spend our entire lives without ever having to endure catastrophic loss of either life or property from a natural disaster. Nor will we be the victim of a violent crime, be persecuted for our faith, be subjected to grinding poverty, or be participants in any number of other grand sufferings that befall humanity. When someone experiences any one of these evils, it is one too many, but in truth, comparatively few have to carry that burden. And those who do usually experience the goodness of mercy and compassion from those committed to easing suffering.

Would you agree with Orwell that "on balance life is suffering"? Why, or why not?

_____

_____

_____

_____

Just hours before His agonizing execution, Jesus spoke some of His last words. What did Jesus say in John 15:11; 16:24; and 17:13?

_____

_____

_____

_____

_____

Do you think Jesus would agree with Orwell's conclusion? Explain.

_____

_____

_____

_____

_____

The fact that there is more goodness than evil in the world makes at least two powerful arguments. First, if goodness exists in the world, then goodness must be intentional, and if goodness is intentional, then intelligence must be behind it. A number of years ago it was not uncommon to see bumper stickers encouraging drivers to practice "random acts of kindness." Nonsense! How do you practice goodness randomly? There is nothing random about being good, which leads to a second truth: if goodness is intentional and comes from an intelligent mind (God's mind), then goodness—not evil and suffering—is normal and natural. Evil is the foul stench of goodness gone rancid, so it stands to reason that goodness has to exist for evil to exist. God doesn't need Satan, but Satan needs God.

Philosopher Eleonore Stump, wrote on this idea of goodness:

> If we taste and see the goodness of God, then the vision of our world that we see in the mirror of evil will look different, too. Start just with the fact of evil in the world, and the problem of evil presents itself forcefully to you. But start with a view of evil and a deep taste of the goodness of God, and you will know that there must be a morally sufficient reason for God to allow evil — not some legal and ultimately unsatisfying sort of reason, but . . . a reason in which true goodness is manifest. People are accustomed to say that Job got no answer to his anguished demand to know why God had afflicted him. But they forget that in the end Job says to God, "now I see you" [see Job 42:5]. If you could see the loving face of a truly good God, you would have an answer to the question why God had afflicted you. When you see the deep love in the face of a person you suppose has betrayed you, you know you were wrong. Whatever happened was done out of love for you by a heart that would never betray you and a mind bent on your good. To answer a mistaken charge of betrayal, someone who loves you can explain the misunderstanding or he can show his face. Sometimes showing his face heals the hurt much faster.[3]

C. S. Lewis wrote about this same idea in *The Lion, the Witch and the Wardrobe* when he spoke of a deeper magic—the truth that the mystery of goodness is deeper than the mystery of evil and suffering.

Starting Your Journey

The mystery of suffering is deeply profound, but the mystery of goodness is deeper still. Why goodness exists in the world is a formidable challenge for those who doubt that God can be good and powerful and allow suffering to exist. Therefore, those who ask about God's goodness and human suffering need more than a philosophical reply; they need practical answers that bring comfort. A three-sided framework is useful as we respond to others as well as to assess the questions for ourselves. On one side are three things we should never do when giving answers; on another side are three things we should always do when giving answers; and on a third side are three things every sufferer wants in the midst of his or her suffering.

What We Should Never Do When Giving Answers

First, *never give answers to foolish questioners*. Some questioners are not seekers of truth but are looking to pick a fight. They engage in debate for the sake of being argumentative—in an attempt to make the faithful look like fools. We should treat these questioners with kindness and respect but refuse to engage in a battle of words. This is the teaching of Proverbs 26:4 which advises that we should not answer those who would attempt to reduce us to the level of a fool. Jesus gave similar advice in Matthew 7:6 when He said, "Do not give what is holy to dogs, and do not throw your pearls before swine, or they will trample them under their feet, and turn and tear you to pieces." Jesus's warning is specifically against presenting the gospel to those aggressively hostile to it because they will scorn the truth and attack the presenter.

On the other hand, Proverbs 26:5 recommends that we help a fool recognize his or her folly; if possible, "Answer a fool in simple terms / so he doesn't get a swelled head" (MSG). It takes wisdom to know when to answer and when to keep silent. In general, however, this rule is worth following: Never wallow with a hog. You both get muddy, but the hog likes it.

If applicable, describe a time in your life when you encountered a questioner who wasn't serious about finding the truth.

_____

_____

_____

_____

_____

_____

How did you handle that person? What did you say?

_____

_____

_____

_____

_____

_____

What was the outcome of that situation? What was the person's response?

_____

_____

_____

_____

Second, *never give answers to questions that are beyond your knowledge*. When it comes to providing answers to the question of evil and suffering, you either have something to say or you don't, and if you don't, then keep quiet. It is simply true that we cannot know what we don't know, and we cannot answer what we don't understand. Saying, "I don't know," requires humility. Humans are questioning creatures, but we are also answering creatures who don't always know how to admit ignorance. When we truly do not know the answer to a question, however, we must swallow our pride and offer a humble, "I don't know."

Let's approach the subject of suffering with a little humility. Answers are not easily come by. We must recognize that human answers will never fully satisfy every human question and questioner, and that some questions are beyond human answers. The reality is,

> Oceans of ink have flowed in search
> of answers to evil [and suffering], but
> no human mind has ever figured it all
> out. The essential mystery remains and
> always will. If there had been a simple
> answer, it would have been found
> by now. Whatever answers we each
> believe to be true will still face further
> questions that they do not answer
> completely.[4]

It may be that we never have answers to our questions. Perhaps this is because we couldn't understand the answers even if they were given. This, then, becomes an act of grace.

Read Job 40:3–5 and 42:1–6. What was Job's response after God questioned him?

_____

_____

_____

_____

Give a little grace to those who ask about God and suffering. If you don't have an answer, hold your tongue.

Third, *never give answers to questions without love.* When Job's three friends sat down next to him on his ash heap, they came with their self-righteousness well hidden. But when they opened their mouths, all doubts about their agenda were dispelled. Their intentions were to set their friend straight, to confront him about his sin, and to motivate him to repent.

But they got everything wrong. They misdiagnosed Job's problem; his calamity wasn't due to a personal, hidden sin. They misunderstood God's sovereignty— that He can't be bought off with corrupted self-righteousness. And they mistook their own theological insight; they didn't know what they were talking about. Their answers didn't relieve the suffering of their friend; instead, their answers inflicted additional pain on his already tortured soul. If we aren't careful, we can become like Job's friends, wounding with callous words and calling it love.

Because Job's friends were wrong about him, about God, and about their own knowledge, their answers were insensitive and cruel. And both Job and God called them out. Read the following passages and summarize what Job and God said and why.

Job 13:4–5

_____

_____

_____

_____

Job 42:7

_____

_____

_____

_____

What did Paul admonish in Colossians 4:5–6?

_____

_____

_____

_____

Describe a modern-day example of a situation in which Paul's advice was not followed. What difference would love have made?

_____

_____

_____

_____

What We Should Always Do When Giving Answers

Number one: *always answer questions with a balance of heart and head.* When confronted with painful realities and difficult questions, it's tempting to answer with our hearts and not our heads. This is especially true in the face of death. We often end up saying things to sufferers that are silly and false, like, "God needed another angel." But no matter how pleasant it sounds, it's simply not true. We don't turn into angels when we die, and God certainly doesn't need another one. Our hearts ensure answers that are loving and sensitive, but our heads ensure answers that are truthful and Christ-honoring. That is the beauty of balance.

Number two: *always give answers that are truthful, even if painful.* This doesn't give us license to be like Job's friends, who were both insensitive and wrong. Marcus Aurelius, the Roman Emperor and Stoic philosopher wrote, "Speak the truth as you see it. But with kindness. With humility. Without hypocrisy."[5] Even better, heed Paul's admonition: speak the truth in love (Ephesians 4:15).

The things all sufferers want immediately are answers to their questions. But answers are not always immediately available. Sufferers don't like to hear that, but they must hear it because they cannot live on false hope. Sometimes answers are revealed and sometimes they're not. The question is, "Can you trust God even if you never know why you suffer?"

Number three: *always give answers that point to the gospel.* When people suffer, we often point them to the book of Job, hoping they (and we) will find answers there. But the book of Job says more about the mysterious sovereignty of God than it does about the meaning of suffering. If we look to Job for the answer to the question of suffering, we must be prepared to discover that the answer is not a why or wherefore but a *who.* And those who suffer only discover the *who* through the fullness and richness of the gospel. Only the cross, the resurrection, and the hope of life anew will fully satisfy the longing and lonely heart. If you'd like some help in presenting this powerful message or if you'd simply like to learn more for yourself, turn to "How to Begin a Relationship with God" on page 77.

What is the great promise found in Romans 8:35, 38–39?

_____

_____

_____

_____

_____

_____

How might this promise bring hope to the hurting?

_____

_____

_____

_____

_____

_____

What Sufferers Want in the Midst of Their Suffering

Sufferers want a silent friend. If we could be transported back to the world of Danish philosopher Søren Kierkegaard, we'd think we had stepped inside a monastery. But to Kierkegaard, his world was just as noisy as ours. He mused, "In view of the present situation of the world . . . one might Christianly say, 'It is a sickness'—and if I were a physician [I would prescribe] silence."[6]

"Silence itself is eloquent sympathy," Os Guinness wrote.[7] We who use too many words should learn such eloquence. Through it, sufferers might hear God.

Read Job 2:12–13. What was the initial response of Job's friends?

_____

_____

_____

_____

What can we learn from this example?

_____

_____

_____

_____

Sufferers want a listening ear. When sufferers ask questions, they aren't always looking for answers; they simply want to release the pressure that suffering brings. It takes discernment and sensitivity to know when to speak and when to remain silent, but when in doubt, be slow to speak and quick to listen (James 1:19).

Simone Weil wrote, "To listen to someone is to put oneself in his place while he is speaking." Weil continued:

> To put oneself in the place of someone whose soul is corroded by affliction, or in near danger of it, is to annihilate oneself. It is more difficult than suicide would be for a happy child. Therefore the afflicted are not listened to. They are like someone whose tongue has been cut out and who occasionally forgets the fact. When they move their lips no ear perceives any sound. And they themselves soon sink into impotence in the use of language, because of the certainty of not being heard.[8]

Talking is easy; listening is hard. But listening is the one thing you must do when you encounter a soul who is suffering. Listen—not to respond but to understand.

Sufferers want a reassuring touch. Great care must be taken when touching; it must be appropriate, gentle, and invited. But great ministry can take place with a simple touch; it offers security, sympathy, and intimacy. In the words of Tennessee Williams, "Devils can be driven out of the heart by the touch of a hand on a hand."[9]

Keeping in mind that Jesus was God incarnate, read the following passages and record the results of Jesus's touch.

Matthew 8:14–15

_____

_____

_____

_____

Matthew 17:6–8

_____

_____

_____

_____

Mark 1:40–42

_____

_____

_____

_____

What might we learn from Jesus's example?

_____

_____

_____

_____

Drawing from what you've learned in this book, jot
down notes, outline several steps, or create a plan on
how you will respond the next time you encounter
someone who is suffering or facing the question of
suffering.

_____

_____

_____

_____

_____

_____

Oskar Schindler saved 1,100 Jews in 1945 . . . as well as whole generations born from them. And yet, some saw Schindler as an evil man because he was a Nazi, worthy of being branded a war criminal. Others, though, saw Schindler as a savior, a man of deep goodness.

So it is with our God—many are conflicted about the goodness of God and the state of the world. Some are contemptuous of God because they look out on the world and see only suffering. Others are consumed with life's pain and seek only comfort. But we, as people of faith, look and see the profound goodness of our God, even in the swirl of suffering. So what do we say to those who aren't able to see what we see?

Answers are not always easy to come by, but whatever answers we give, we must point people to the deeper mystery of goodness in the world—the goodness of the gospel. We must point them to this essential truth: *God's answer to suffering is not a philosophy but a Person, not something but Someone, not a word but the Word, not a myth but the Messiah, not commentary but the cross, not human reason but divine resurrection. God's answer is Jesus Christ.*

My Questions and Thoughts

My Questions and Thoughts

How to Begin a Relationship with God

Everyone who has been cast into the darkness of suffering knows the disquieting reality that life as they once knew it is now indistinguishable. Like wandering in a darkened wood, life no longer provides reliable signposts to steer a confused soul. The human soul cannot survive without direction—without hope. Many people turn to philosophies or pleasures in attempts to find answers and to ease their suffering. But their efforts are in vain. Hope for hurting lives will never be found in philosophies or pleasures but in a Person—the person of Jesus Christ. And He can be found only by walking the path of faith. The Bible marks this path with four essential truths. Let's look at each marker in detail.

Our Spiritual Condition: Totally Corrupt

The first truth is rather personal. One look in the mirror of Scripture, and our human condition becomes painfully clear:

> "There is none righteous, not even one;
> There is none who understands,
> There is none who seeks for God;
> All have turned aside, together they
>   have become useless;

There is none who does good,
There is not even one."
(Romans 3:10–12)

We are all sinners through and through—totally
depraved. Now, that doesn't mean we've committed
every atrocity known to humankind. We're not as *bad* as
we can be, just as *bad off* as we can be. Sin colors all our
thoughts, motives, words, and actions.

If you've been around a while, you likely already
believe it. Look around. Everything around us bears the
smudge marks of our sinful nature. Despite our best
efforts to create a perfect world, crime statistics continue
to soar, divorce rates keep climbing, and families keep
crumbling.

Something has gone terribly wrong in our society
and in ourselves—something deadly. Contrary to how
the world would repackage it, "me-first" living doesn't
equal rugged individuality and freedom; it equals death.
As Paul said in his letter to the Romans, "The wages of
sin is death" (6:23)—our spiritual and physical death
that comes from God's righteous judgment of our sin,
along with all of the emotional and practical effects of
this separation that we experience on a daily basis. This
brings us to the second marker: God's character.

God's Character: Infinitely Holy

How can God judge us for a sinful state we were born
into? Our total depravity is only half the answer. The
other half is God's infinite holiness.

The fact that we know things are not as they
should be points us to a standard of goodness beyond
ourselves. Our sense of injustice in life on this side of
eternity implies a perfect standard of justice beyond our

reality. That standard and source is God Himself. And God's standard of holiness contrasts starkly with our sinful condition.

Scripture says that "God is Light, and in Him there is no darkness at all" (1 John 1:5). God is absolutely holy—which creates a problem for us. If He is so pure, how can we who are so impure relate to Him?

Perhaps we could try being better people, try to tilt the balance in favor of our good deeds, or seek out methods for self-improvement. Throughout history, people have attempted to live up to God's standard by keeping the Ten Commandments or living by their own code of ethics. Unfortunately, no one can come close to satisfying the demands of God's law. Romans 3:20 says, "By the works of the Law no flesh will be justified in His sight; for through the Law comes the knowledge of sin."

Our Need: A Substitute

So here we are, sinners by nature and sinners by choice, trying to pull ourselves up by our own bootstraps to attain a relationship with our holy Creator. But every time we try, we fall flat on our faces. We can't live a good enough life to make up for our sin, because God's standard isn't "good enough"—it's *perfection*. And we can't make amends for the offense our sin has created without dying for it.

Who can get us out of this mess?

If someone could live perfectly, honoring God's law, and would bear sin's death penalty for us—in our place—then we would be saved from our predicament. But is there such a person? Thankfully, yes!

Meet your substitute—*Jesus Christ*. He is the One who took death's place for you!

> [God] made [Jesus Christ] who knew
> no sin to be sin on our behalf, so that
> we might become the righteousness of
> God in Him. (2 Corinthians 5:21)

God's Provision: A Savior

God rescued us by sending His Son, Jesus, to die on the cross for our sins (1 John 4:9–10). Jesus was fully human and fully divine (John 1:1, 18), a truth that ensures His understanding of our weaknesses, His power to forgive, and His ability to bridge the gap between God and us (Romans 5:6–11). In short, we are "justified as a gift by His grace through the redemption which is in Christ Jesus" (3:24). Two words in this verse bear further explanation: *justified* and *redemption*.

Justification is God's act of mercy, in which He declares righteous the believing sinners while we are still in our sinning state. Justification doesn't mean that God *makes* us righteous, so that we never sin again, rather that He *declares* us righteous — much like a judge pardons a guilty criminal. Because Jesus took our sin upon Himself and suffered our judgment on the cross, God forgives our debt and proclaims us PARDONED.

Redemption is Christ's act of paying the complete price to release us from sin's bondage. God sent His Son to bear His wrath for all of our sins — past, present, and future (Romans 3:24–26; 2 Corinthians 5:21). In humble obedience, Christ willingly endured the shame of the cross for our sake (Mark 10:45; Romans 5:6–8; Philippians 2:8). Christ's death satisfied God's righteous demands. He no longer holds our sins against us, because His own Son paid the penalty for them. We are freed from the slave market of sin, never to be enslaved again!

Placing Your Faith in Christ

These four truths describe how God has provided a way to Himself through Jesus Christ. Because the price has been paid in full by God, we must respond to His free gift of eternal life in total faith and confidence in Him to save us. We must step forward into the relationship with God that He has prepared for us—not by doing good works or by being a good person, but by coming to Him just as we are and accepting His justification and redemption by faith.

> For by grace you have been saved through faith; and that not of your-selves, it is the gift of God; not as a result of works, so that no one may boast. (Ephesians 2:8–9)

We accept God's gift of salvation simply by placing our faith in Christ alone for the forgiveness of our sins. Would you like to enter a relationship with your Creator by trusting in Christ as your Savior? If so, here's a simple prayer you can use to express your faith:

> *Dear God,*
>
> *I know that my sin has put a barrier between You and me. Thank You for sending Your Son, Jesus, to die in my place. I trust in Jesus alone to forgive my sins, and I accept His gift of eternal life. I ask Jesus to be my personal Savior and the Lord of my life. Thank You. In Jesus's name, amen.*

If you've prayed this prayer or one like it and you wish to find out more about knowing God and His plan for you in the Bible, contact us at Insight for Living. Our contact information is on the following pages.

We Are Here for You

If you desire to find out more about knowing God and His plan for you in the Bible, contact us. Insight for Living provides staff pastors who are available for free written correspondence or phone consultation. These seminary-trained and seasoned counselors have years of experience and are well-qualified guides for your spiritual journey.

Please feel welcome to contact your regional Pastoral Ministries by using the information below:

United States

Insight for Living
Pastoral Ministries
Post Office Box 269000
Plano, Texas 75026-9000
USA
972-473-5097, Monday through Friday,
8:00 a.m. – 5:00 p.m. central time
www.insight.org/contactapastor

Canada

Insight for Living Canada
Pastoral Ministries
Post Office Box 2510
Vancouver, BC V6B 3W7
CANADA
1-800-663-7639
info@insightforliving.ca

Australia, New Zealand, and South Pacific

Insight for Living Australia
Pastoral Care
Post Office Box 443
Boronia, VIC 3155
AUSTRALIA
1 300 467 444

United Kingdom and Europe

Insight for Living United Kingdom
Pastoral Care
PO Box 553
Dorking
RH4 9EU
UNITED KINGDOM
0800 915 9364
+44 (0)1306 640156
pastoralcare@insightforliving.org.uk

Endnotes

Opening Quote

1. Alister E. McGrath, *The Journey: A Pilgrim in the Lands of the Spirit*, 1st ed. (New York: Doubleday, 2000), 21–22.

Chapter 1

Adapted from "Hope Beyond Suffering: How We Can Smile Through Suffering," chapter two in Charles R. Swindoll's book *Hope Again: When Life Hurts and Dreams Fade* (Dallas: Word Publishing, 1996), 11–23. Used by permission.

1. Warren W. Wiersbe, *Be Hopeful* (Wheaton, Ill.: SP Publications, Victor Books, 1988), 11.

2. H. L. Mencken, *A Mencken Chrestomathy* (New York: Knopf, 1949), 617.

3. Wiersbe, *Be Hopeful*, 14–15.

4. James Moffatt, *The General Epistles: James, Peter, and Judas* (London: Hodder and Stoughton, 1963), 95.

5. C. S. Lewis, *The Problem of Pain*, in *The Complete C. S. Lewis Signature Classics* (San Francisco: HarperSanFrancisco, 2002), 407.

6. Frederick William Danker, ed., *A Greek-English Lexicon of the New Testament and other Early Christian Literature*, rev. 3d ed. (Chicago: University of Chicago Press, 2000), 842.

7. Julie Ackerman Link, "Fully Involved in the Flame," in *Seasons: A Journal for the Women of Calvary Church*, Spring 1996, 1. Copyright Calvary Church, Grand Rapids, Michigan.

Chapter 2

Adapted from the message "A Soul Drenched in Tears: Why Me and How Do I Endure?" from the series, *Enigma: Wrestling with Evil and Suffering* by Derrick G. Jeter, Coffee House Fellowship, Stonebriar Community Church, Frisco, Texas, November 8, 2009. Copyright © 2009 by Derrick G. Jeter. All rights reserved worldwide. Used by permission.

1. Elliot Roosevelt to Corinne Roosevelt, quoted in Edmund Morris, *The Rise of Theodore Roosevelt* (New York: Coward, McCann & Geoghegan, 1979), 240.

2. Theodore Roosevelt, quoted in Morris, *The Rise of Theodore Roosevelt*, 241.

3. Theodore Roosevelt, quoted in Morris, *The Rise of Theodore Roosevelt*, 241.

4. N. T. Wright, *Evil and the Justice of God* (Downers Grove, Ill.: InterVarsity, 2006), 23–24.

5. Friedrich Nietzsche, *Twilight of the Idols: Or, How to Philosophize with the Hammer*, trans. Richard Polt (Indianapolis: Hackett, 1997), 6.

6. Dante Alighieri, "Inferno," 3.9, in *The Divine Comedy*, trans. Allen Mandelbaum (New York: Everyman's Library, Alfred A. Knoph, 1995), 68.

7. Simone Weil, "The Love of God and Affliction," in *Waiting for God*, trans. Emma Craufurd (New York: Perennial Classics, 2001), 73.

8. C. S. Lewis, *A Grief Observed*, in *The Complete C. S. Lewis Signature Classics* (San Francisco: HarperSanFrancisco, 2002), 443–44.

9. Kenneth S. Wuest, "Hebrews: In the Greek New Testament," in *Wuest's Word Studies: From the Greek New Testament*, vol. 2 (Grand Rapids: Eerdmans, 1973), 235.

10. John Donne, "XVII *Nunc Lento Sonitu Dicunt*, Morieris," in *Donne: Poems and Prose* (New York: Everyman's Library, Alfred A. Knoph, 1995), 227.

11. *Wit*, DVD, directed by Mike Nichols (New York: Home Box Office, 2001).

Chapter 3

Adapted from "What Job Teaches Us about Ourselves," chapter twenty-one in Charles R. Swindoll's book *Job: A Man of Heroic Endurance* (Nashville: W Publishing Group, 2004), 321–38. Used by permission.

1. "How to Decide Who to Marry?" http://ozjokes.com/jokes /32-kids/180-how-to-decide-who-to-marry, accessed February 24, 2010.

2. Rosamund Stone Zander and Benjamin Zander, *The Art of Possibility* (Boston: Harvard Business School Press, 2000), 118–19.

3. Francis I. Andersen, *Job: An Introduction and Commentary*, Tyndale Old Testament Commentaries (Downers Grove, Ill.: InterVarsity, 1976), 93–94.

4. Charles M. Schulz, *Peanuts* cartoon, quoted in Robert L. Short, *The Parables of Peanuts* (New York: Harper & Row, 1968), 246–47. Peanuts: © United Feature Syndicate, Inc.

5. Oswald Chambers, "The Sacrament of the Saint," in *My Utmost for His Highest: Selections for the Year* (Uhrichsville, Ohio: Barbour, 1963), August 10.

Chapter 4

Adapted from the message "A Deeper Mystery: What Do We Say to Those Who Ask?" from the series, *Enigma: Wrestling with Evil and Suffering* by Derrick G. Jeter, Coffee House Fellowship, Stonebriar Community Church, Frisco, Texas, November 15, 2009. Copyright © 2009 by Derrick G. Jeter. All rights reserved worldwide. Used by permission.

1. *Schindler's List*, DVD, directed by Steven Spielberg (1993; Universal City, Calif.: Universal Pictures, 2004).

2. George Orwell, "Lear, Tolstoy and the Fool," in *Essays* (New York: Everyman's Library, Alfred A. Knopf, 2002), 1196.

3. Eleonore Stump, "The Mirror of Evil," in *God and the Philosophers: The Reconciliation of Faith and Reason*, ed. Thomas V. Morris (New York: Oxford University Press, 1994), 242.

4. Os Guinness, *Unspeakable: Facing Up to Evil in an Age of Genocide and Terror* (San Francisco: HarperSanFrancisco, 2005), 199.

5. Marcus Aurelius, *Meditations*, 8.5, trans. Gregory Hays (New York: Modern Library, 2002), 102.

6. Søren Kierkegaard, "The Mirror of the Word," in *For Self-Examination and Judge for Yourselves! and Three Discourses*, trans. Walter Lowrie (Princeton, N.J.: Princeton University Press, 1944), 71.

7. Guinness, *Unspeakable*, 205.

8. Simone Weil, "Human Personality," in *Simone Weil: An Anthology*, ed. Siân Miles (New York: Grove Press, 1986), 71.

9. Tennessee Williams, *The Milk Train Doesn't Stop Here Anymore*, scene 5 (New York: Dramatists Play Service, 1964), 62.

Resources for Probing Further

More ink has been spilled on the issue of evil and suffering than perhaps any other issue in human history. Because this is almost certainly true, the book you hold in your hands doesn't pretend to be *the* answer to the difficult questions of why a good God allows suffering and how we can find hope when all looks hopeless. This book is merely a primer to spur your thinking and to offer a glimpse of hope. Obviously, we cannot provide an exhaustive list of resources on suffering here, but we do recommend the following books to further your study of this profound topic. Please keep in mind, we cannot always endorse everything a writer or ministry says in these works, so we encourage you to approach these and all other nonbiblical resources with wisdom and discernment.

Alcorn, Randy. *If God Is Good: Faith in the Midst of Suffering and Evil.* Colorado Springs: Multnomah, 2009.

Guinness, Os. *Unspeakable: Facing Up to Evil in an Age of Genocide and Terror.* San Francisco: HarperSanFrancisco, 2005.

Hart, David Bentley. *The Doors of the Sea: Where Was God in the Tsunami?* Grand Rapids: Eerdmans, 2005.

Kreeft, Peter. *Making Sense Out of Suffering*. Ann Arbor: Servant, 1986.

Lewis, C. S. *A Grief Observed*. New York: HarperCollins, 2001.

Lewis, C. S. *The Problem of Pain*. New York: HarperCollins, 2001.

Piper, John, and Justin Taylor, eds. *Suffering and the Sovereignty of God*. Wheaton, Ill.: Crossway, 2006.

Swindoll, Charles R. *Hope Again: When Life Hurts and Dreams Fade*. Dallas: W Publishing, 1996.

Swindoll, Charles R. *Job: A Man of Heroic Endurance*. Nashville: W Publishing, 2004.

Wiersbe, Warren W. *Why Us? When Bad Things Happen to God's People*. Old Tappan, N.J.: Revell, 1984.

Wright, N. T. *Evil and the Justice of God*. Downers Grove, Ill.: InterVarsity, 2006.

Ordering Information

If you would like to order additional copies of
Hope for the Hurting or order other Insight for Living
resources, please contact the office that serves you

United States

United States
Insight for Living
Post Office Box 269000
Plano, Texas 75026-9000
USA
1-800-772-8888 (Monday through Friday,
7:00 a.m. –7:00 p.m. central time)
www.insight.org
www.insightworld.org

Canada

Insight for Living Canada
Post Office Box 2510
Vancouver, BC V6B 3W7
CANADA
1-800-663-7639
www.insightforliving.ca

Australia, New Zealand, and South Pacific

Insight for Living Australia
Post Office Box 443
Boronia, VIC 3155
AUSTRALIA
1 300 467 444
www.insight.asn.au

United Kingdom and Europe

Insight for Living United Kingdom
PO Box 553
Dorking
RH4 9EU
UNITED KINGDOM
0800 915 9364
www.insightforliving.org.uk

Other International Locations

International constituents may contact the U.S. office
through our Web site (www.insightworld.org), mail
queries, or by calling +1-972-473-5136.